LARNA

LIVING IN THE
Spirit of God

LitPrime Solutions
21250 Hawthorne Blvd
Suite 500, Torrance, CA 90503
www.litprime.com
Phone: 1-800-981-9893

© 2024 Larna. All rights reserved.

No part of this book may be reproduced, stored in a retrieval system, or transmitted by any means without the written permission of the author.

Published by LitPrime Solutions   01/09/2024

ISBN: 979-8-88703-337-2(sc)
ISBN: 979-8-88703-338-9(e)

Library of Congress Control Number: 2023924112

Any people depicted in stock imagery provided by iStock are models, and such images are being used for illustrative purposes only.

Certain stock imagery © iStock.

Because of the dynamic nature of the Internet, any web addresses or links contained in this book may have changed since publication and may no longer be valid. The views expressed in this work are solely those of the author and do not necessarily reflect the views of the publisher, and the publisher hereby disclaims any responsibility for them.

Dedicated to Ms. Lena Amonte, Spiritualist.

I'm dedicating portions of my knowledge to a lady whom I knew at an early age in Grand Rapids, Michigan. I give thanks to God and her for all the help. She continually told me that what she had for me was a gift from God. Ms. Amonte helped me understand what I was going through at that time in my life, which was something that—I now know—was nothing short of God's miracles. Through the help of God, I was able to see the light at the end of the tunnel. Although she has long passed away, I have heard from her through mediumship. God is still using her to help in bringing me knowledge, encouragement, and understanding.

Introduction
Living in the Spirit of "God"

Volume one is an introduction to the spiritual visions of Larna Woods. It explores the life of Ms. Woods as she progresses in curiosity, age, faith, belief, and the many avenues that may be followed and learned from the spirit world. Ms. Woods hopes that you will learn and enjoy the stories that are illustrated by her. Stories of miracles and the other volumes of stories that will follow in the future.

Chapter One
First Friends

As a very young child, I was always told that I was strange. I grew up in a very strict family. My father was the son of a Baptist minister from the south, West Virginia. My mother was the daughter of a housekeeper mother and a father who worked for the railroad. Mother was very strict as to what to do as a lady and what not to do. My father believed that children were to be seen and not heard. What children have to say meant little if not anything; feelings were not taken into consideration.

I don't remember how or when it all started with my spiritual friends. I have a lot of people around me—there are many brothers and sisters in my life. With my father being very harsh, there were a lot of beatings with whatever you would like to call the instruments, lots of yelling and screaming, mostly from my father. Mother did her share also but she wasn't much of a screamer. Both my parents like to be strict. I guess that's how they showed the sign of strength to their children in those days. I grew up scared of making him or her angry. Maybe this having spiritual friends was my way of escaping the harshness of that childhood. I have to admit, though, that having my spiritual friends made my childhood much more bearable. My spiritual friends and I had lots of fun, especially at night when everyone else would be asleep. We children had strict bedtime rules. When we went to bed, it was in bed and no noise.

I did the same as the other children. But as soon as I would go to sleep and my other sisters and brothers were asleep, my little spiritual friend would wake me up. Sometimes it would be to talk about what was bothering me or to play a game with me. We played games like hide and seek, Jacks, and peekaboo—it was fun. I would actually hide from my spiritual friends and they would look for me and vice versa. I could see them peeking around corners from me. This was usually about 2:30 or 3:30 in the morning. I would be in all parts of the basement. When we played Jacks, I would watch and play along with them. There were usually three or four children including myself.

If I did something wrong, they would tell me it wasn't the right thing to do. They would often tell me that I had to do the right thing by apologizing or telling the truth about the situation. One time, I did something very bad. Then they came to me and told me that if I didn't tell my parents the truth that I was the one who did it, my parents would whip all of us. And that would not be the right thing. They told me to tell my father and that he would not do anything to me. So I went upstairs. My father was in the living room, sitting in his chair, reading his Sunday newspaper. I just stood there for a minute then I told my father what I had done.

He stated, "You did that, did you?"

I told him, "yes," and that I wanted to apologize for my actions. I told him that I was sorry about what happened and that I hope that he will forgive me for doing wrong.

My father looked at me in disbelief and said, "You're sorry?"

I said, "Yes."

He immediately rushed from the living room to the kitchen where my mother was preparing dinner. I heard my father tell my mother what I said.

My mother said to my father, "James, you know how she is. She not like the other children. Just leave her alone."

My father came from the kitchen looking at me in a puzzled way and told me to go back to bed. And that was that.

Often, during the night, I would wake my sisters up to come play with my spiritual friends and me. Needless to say, they would refuse. They claimed that they could not see my friends. I remember one night in particular that my spiritual friends and I went to my sisters' bedroom and asked them to get up and play. When I pointed to them, my sister said that she couldn't see them or hear them. I thought everybody could see and hear them like I did. My spiritual friends told me that they were standing next to me and that my sisters couldn't see them. I couldn't understand that because they were real to me. Years later, my sister was telling the same story to some friends of the family when we were discussing spiritual happenings. She said that she remembered all the times I would come to their bedroom and asked them to play. She also said that she couldn't hear or see them, but that I would be talking and playing games all by myself. My spiritual friends were there for me if I needed help at any time. They comforted me, played with me, and told me the right from wrong things to do, and taught me many things.

My spiritual friends were with me all the time that I lived there until we moved from a very large, three-story Victorian house on the city's northwest side to a small house in the suburbs. After that time, I don't remember them being around, so it could be that they were just in the house when we moved there. They were there all the years that we live in the big Victorian house. After we moved, I never saw those spiritual friends again. I really missed them. I would stay awake at night waiting for them to appear, but they never came again.

Chapter Two
It Had To Be "God"

Time went by somewhat unnoticed by many unusual dreams and visions. By this time, my mother was pregnant again with my precious brother who was the fourth boy of the family. His name was Jimmy. During the time of my mother's pregnancy, I had many dreams that were about the coming of my little brother. I had dreamed that I would have to care for him and protect him until he reached a certain age—before puberty I guess. This was almost like a haunting thought in my daily life; it truly engulfed me. As the years went by, I had vision after vision of his demise at a truly early age. Years went by, and I became more of a mother to him than an older sister. I love him so much.

While we were about to move to the suburbs, I was taken to Cincinnati, Ohio to help take care of an elderly woman whose name was Sister Dorcas. This was my second time being there with this lady. The first time, I got homesick and they sent me back home to Michigan. This woman was a cousin of my mother's. She was in her late eighties at the time. She was a nun. Her given name was Sister Dorcas. I believe she was having some form of dementia at the time. Sister Dorcas didn't think girls should play in the gym. I was the athletic type. I love playing sports. This just about killed me.

I couldn't have friends with long hair because they were sinners, so it was hard. It was a hard road to travel for a fourteen-year-old girl. It was pretty bad. I just stayed away from home as much as possible. I met a friend who went to the same school. She was okay, but she treated me like I didn't know anything because I was from the north, a little country town. I just went along with it most of the time. Besides, I like her brother. I guess I had a crush on him, so I kind of hung out with her and some friends. At any rate, this gave me somewhere to be until my curfew time 10:00 pm.

In my first stay in Cincinnati, there wasn't much fun at all. I just stayed inside unless I went to my cousin's. There was a lot of downtime for me that included homesickness, wanting to be with friends, and a familiar territory. It was during my second stay in Cincinnati, when I was about fourteen years old, I wanted to get away from home. Life was unbearable, not to mention school and all its prejudices. I somewhat made a deal with my mother to let me go back to Cincinnati, Ohio. So she gave me permission to go and take care of Sister Dorcas once again. Many people patronize her for her dealings in potions and many kinds of other things that I didn't understand. I didn't really know much about it all. I didn't think much about it at the time. I didn't understand it. And what I don't understand, I generally leave alone.

As time went by, life appeared to be a little more bearable. I would just make it home in time to get to bed for the night. This would save me from conversations with Sister Dorcas about my goings and comings. One night, on my way home, I was on my way through the park entrance instead of walking around as I had always done before. When I stepped onto the pavement entering the park, I heard a loud male voice say to me, "Stop!"

Again I said to myself, *Okay, Larna, here we go again.* I'm hearing things. I looked around to see where this man's voice was coming from, but there was no one there. I thought to myself, *It's just me, hearing things.* I proceeded to the gate of the park when something grabbed me by the shoulders. I felt the pressure of its hands holding me. I began to move, not by myself but by this spiritual entity. I couldn't feel my feet on the sidewalk. I was looking around, wondering what was happening as I was moved around the park. It seemed so unreal. It didn't make sense to be walking around the park when all I needed to do is cut through from gate to gate. This continued until the entity walked me up five flights of stairs, and in front of the apartment door that I lived in with Sister Dorcas. I felt the release of the pressure from its hold on me on my upper arms. In a daze, I shook my head as if to come out of it. Then I proceeded in through the door.

The next morning, as I was getting dressed for school and listening to the radio news. I heard of a body that was reportedly found in the same park. It was concluded that the young girl had been killed around the time that I would have been in that park the night before. It was so unreal. I prayed and thanked God for the protection that he has given me. So many times I have been protected this way, but I never knew why. Now I know that I have work to do and lots of it. Now I know why God has spared me as he has others. I'm sure of this.

Chapter Three
The Nun's Visit

The next amazing thing that happened one fall afternoon was that a friendly young nun came to visit. I had not seen her until this time. She was very nice. When I came into the apartment, I didn't know that she was there. And not to interrupt them, I just pulled out my books and began to study. This nun was there for about an hour, and I was still studying my history lesson. The nun was repeatedly watching me. This I could not figure out why. I did everything as usual, wiping the sweat from my hands and piling the towels up on the floor by my chair as I studied. Finally, the nun interrupted me. She asked me what was wrong with my hands. I replied that there was nothing wrong and that my hands were always sweating like this. After telling that to the nun, she immediately began to pray for me. At that point, I began to get somewhat upset, thinking to myself that something was gravely wrong with me.

She noticed my expression and said right away, "There was nothing wrong, honey." She proceeded to ask me how long had this been happening.

I replied, "All my life."

She asked Sister Dorcas if she had noticed my hands sweating like that before. I heard Sister Dorcas tell the nun "yes." At that point, the young nun said that she had heard about it and had read about it, but had never experienced it herself until now.

At this point, she asked if she could see my hands. She held my hand and then wipe away the sweat. Of course, my hands just continued to sweat. She said a prayer and just looked at me. Then she said that God has something to tell me. She told me not to be alarmed but that, in several years my hands will stop sweating and God was going to let me know why my hands sweat and what type of gift God had given me. And when it happens, she said, I would know what I have to do with it—the gift.

Chapter Four
Time to Move Ahead

It's been months since I've been able to write for this first volume. Really, nearly a year has passed since I started writing. I sat and prayed most days for the spirit of God to give me what I needed to say. The next story for my volume—was it the story that I was thinking of or what? I had been having trouble writing or getting started on this chapter. This chapter was supposed to be about my younger brother, Jimmy, who met a fatal accident when he was just seven years old, the situations leading up to it, and the spiritual directions and involvement. It was hard for me to put my mind around all that had happened and remembering him. But this morning was different. The day started different, it even looked different and felt different.

It happened this morning. The sun appeared bright and even brighter than before. The morning seemed so quiet, no noise. I felt better than I had in many months, and I just wondered what I'm going to do today. I had breakfast, got situated for the day's daily living activities, and settled back to relax for the day. But I was still wondering, what is it that I can do today? Why is it taking me so long to finish this chapter? I wondered around my small apartment and finally stopped in my bedroom at the bed. I was sitting on the end of the bed, when all of a sudden, I heard a child's voice say, *"You can write it now."*

At that point, I wasn't sure whether I had actually heard the voice or not. Then I said to myself, *Did I hear that?*

The voice came again, *"You can write it now."*

I believe at that time that it was the voice of my younger brother, Jimmy. It was such a thrill to hear his soft young voice.

I immediately took my papers and began to write after about a year of trying. This was so good. The writings and thoughts just flowed from my mind. It was as if I was being directed as to what and how to write this chapter of this volume. I wrote for hours, not getting stuck on what was to come next or what to write next. It was a beautiful experience. I learned later that this is called spiritual writing, where a spirit directs the course of what is to be written. I continued throughout the day, only taking time out for those necessary things. I would go and continue on without interruptions. The whole experience was beautiful. I finished the next chapter about 9:30 that night. I wondered what had happened and gave thanks to the Holy Spirit of God. I'm continuously thanking God for these miracles and all the others to come in the future.

Chapter Five
The Vision

The visions of my brother's death weeks leading up to it were unnerving. Shortly after my seventeenth birthday, I started having dreams; more like visions. These were all about my younger brother, Jimmy. The vision started with a beautiful day. Not the ordinary beautiful day, but one of events that will be forever remembered. The sun was especially bright—not hot or burning, but bright. Then there would come into focus some issues or irritable situations that I couldn't shake, not knowing what this all meant. I tried to shake it off so it wouldn't change my thought to have a pleasant dream. All of a sudden, things would change to a warning, feeling of concern about my younger brother, Jimmy. I could see him standing there in front of me while I laid on the couch, hands in his pockets and just standing there, looking at me. I remembered telling him about the barbecue we were going to have on the day it all happened.

In the visions, I could see him floating, going down, down, deeper into the pond, as his breath went out of his body. I had also seen him walking into the pond. Walking on until he walked off the man-made cliff. It was a morning not unlike thousands of others, except that the day looked so different. I followed him around like a little puppy until he asked me that morning, "Why are you walking and following me around?"

It was like I was attached to him. In many ways, I was—my heart and soul—that's the way I felt. As I watched Jimmy, a voice came to me as strong and direct and in control of the situation. I thought about how I couldn't take Jimmy with me. I would need to look for another job and pick up my check from the other part-time job I had. I shook my head because I heard a deep voice, a demanding voice. The voice told me to leave him. After that, after hearing the voice, I decided that it wouldn't be a good idea to take him with me. It would be too hectic. He was so young and small for his age. I felt that he wouldn't be able to keep up with me. I decided to do what the voice said. I left him home. He went to Bible school that morning, and, after a brief augment with my parents, I continued with my day.

I wasn't sure at first, but later in the day, I got to thinking about staying in. I suddenly started to go over the details of the vision that I had been having for the last two weeks. I became more and more aware of what was about to happen as the time of the days went by. I started to become very concerned and started to try to hurry things at the mall to get back to the house before something happens, which was in the visions. I started to pray over and over, asking God, *"Please let everything be okay. Please don't take my little brother from me, from us, from my family."* I was rushing by this time, making my way to my part-time job at Montgomery Wards to pick up my paycheck.

I made my way to the downtown Woolworth's. As I was waiting on the buses, it seemed like it was taking me so long to get back home. I was feeling a sensation in my body. I had started to cry. As tears ran down my face, I became more and more anxious. It was like I was losing something inside. It was getting later in the day, and I had to hurry to be back home now. Suddenly, I felt a pull on my heart. It was like a rope or string being pulled through my body—straight from my heart to the bottom of my feet. I could feel the situation of the movement going through my body. I said to myself, *What could this be? What do this mean?* I got up from my seat as the bus stopped in front of Woolworth's. Reluctantly, I moved toward the front of the bus to get off. But there it seemed to be some kind of force that was holding me. I finally reached the steps. As I descended the steps, I felt the force of something. It seemed to be a huge hand in my chest holding me in place. I couldn't move; I just stood there. The people moved around me as they descended the bus. The thought entered my head, *Oh, God, there is nothing to go in the store for. I got the present that I promised little Jimmy*. Forcefully, I pushed on through the store. The first thing I heard was to look at the time on the clock over the door. I turned around and looked at the clock. The time was 6:00 pm. I heard the voice. He was gone now. Something was happening at that very moment...to little Jimmy...but what? All I knew was what I had seen it might be. I prayed and prayed and prayed and prayed again.

I retrieved what I needed and hurried out of the store to get home. I bought a watch for little Jimmy and some candy bars for the other kids. I was so frantic by this time that I could hardly stand up. It seems as if it had taken hours for the bus to come. In reality, it only took fifteen minutes, but it seemed like a lifetime. It was such a long ride to the suburbs where we lived. We lived, twenty-minute drive in a car on the highway from downtown to our home. I knew in my heart that something had indeed happened to my little brother. There's no doubt in my mind at this time.

By the time the bus pulled into the bus stop, I hurried. I ran as fast as I could I'd have to say that I wasn't going to stop. I was just running and running and running, trying to make it home to my little brother, to save him from whatever, from death, or something I didn't understand at the time and still not fully till this day. I have a problem understanding *why*. As I ran, I didn't hear or see the minister of the chapel driving alongside me as I ran up the gravel road. He was yelling at me, and I had to stop awhile to comprehend that he was trying to get my attention. I heard him ask me, "Do you want a ride?" I stated that I was in a hurry, and that I couldn't take the time to talk to him. He was asking me about the family. I couldn't make out what he was saying because of my concern for my brother. I must've appeared to be very ill-mannered at the time. It was all so very blurred. It was like I couldn't hear, I couldn't talk. I could only concentrate on one thing and that was the vision that I had been having for so many weeks. While trying to prevent anything from happening to my little brother, I knew it had happened. I knew he was gone. But I could not accept it.

Finally, I thought that the minister was bothering me, so I accepted the ride. The ride so slow, it felt like the car was moving at a snail's pace. I jumped out the car as the minister was saying that he would take me down the road to the house. I just couldn't wait. I ran to the house and opened the door. The house was silent and still, something I didn't remember hearing before. It was so unusual. It didn't seemed natural for our house to be so quiet; a house full of children. I could feel that there was life that had gone somewhere else. I decided to wait. And I prayed for little Jimmy. Maybe he was with the older boys having a good time. But I knew in my heart that it wasn't true. When the oldest boy came in and put something on the kitchen shelf, I got up to see what it was. It was Jimmy's shirt and glasses. I knew beyond a doubt that he was gone at that point. I proceeded to get the phone and called the police to have them get my brother. Next, I had to find my mother. I had no idea where she was. I prayed and asked God to give me the phone number to find my mother. A phone number appeared in the air and I wrote it down twice on my bus schedule two ways. I called the first number. It wasn't it. Then I tried the second phone number. I was unsure of what I saw with it the first time. I asked the lady, which I knew was my mother's friend, if my mother was there. She answered, "Where did you get my number?" I told her that I couldn't talk. I had to talk to my mother right away. My mother was so angry with me when she got to the phone. I just ignored that. I got right to the point. I told my mother that Jimmy was dead and that he had drowned. I then just hung up the phone and proceeded to call the police to have them get him out of the water.

The police did their best, when they came, to convince me that little Jimmy just out and was playing around with his friends. They used the blow horn and they traveled the neighborhood. When the policeman asked me why did I think he was in the pond. I answered by telling him what I just know. At about 10:00 PM, the police decided to drag the pond. At that time, they found him and came to tell my mom that they got him. At the mention of this, I went into the bathroom to reflect on what had been told to me so many years ago. As I put my hands to my face, I realized that my hands were dry. They were completely dry. At this point, my first thought was, and I realize, that what the nun in Cincinnati had said had came true. When this event took place, she said that my hands would stop sweating and that I would know beyond a doubt what I was put here to do—God's work! Prophesying the word that there is a spirit of God! The time after this realization has been sometimes pleasant. Sometimes it has been difficult, but all in all, it has made me believe that there is indeed a spirit of God!

Chapter Six
The Man from Somewhere

To start with, it was a very cold day in February, around 1964. I had gone back to Cincinnati to care for my mother's cousin who was in her late eighties. Things had not gone well between us, and I begin living with an aunt of mine. This Aunt Lois belonged to a Hoiliness church in the heart of downtown, on Liberty Street. As things would have it, with me being a teenager, we were having difficult days also. I guess it was because of my being a teenager in a new place and all of that as we know it. I had to abide by my aunt's rules. I didn't understand the Hoiliness church. It really scared me more than anything, but I had to go to this program because that's what she wanted. The music was mesmerizing. It made me feel like dancing in the church, but I didn't do it being raised a Baptist. I didn't understand how some people would be in a trance. It seemed that during the entire service, we would sometimes go to break for lunch and return to the church, only to find a young child still in trance and dancing about. So, as you may concur, this is all a bit unusual, to say the least. So, I had a problem going this particular evening when my aunt said that I had to go.

It was a storefront church—those buildings in a long block of buildings that are all build right next to one another. There's no space in between them. As we entered the building, the whole room was freezing. The coal or wood stove had just started to light up. Your breath appeared as white steam as you breathe in the room. It was just that cold. I had on a shepherd coat, the one with tan outside and wool lining inside. But that didn't seem to keep out the chill very well. My hands were cold, my feet were cold. Maybe I was so cold because I was nervous about the evening, not knowing what to expect from this gathering. It was my first of this kind.

The gentleman entered the room, stepped upon the platform, and looked at me. The first thing that came to my mind were questions about why God would send a white man to talk or preach to a group of people in such a church and in such an area. There were hardly any one in the place. Out of the man's mouth, he said that God has sent me here from someplace in Africa to prophecy and help the people here at this church. This scared me so much that I convinced myself that he had to be reading my mind or something. He said that God makes no difference in what color he is or us. He looked at me again. By this time, I'm about out of my skin. He proceeded to point out to some man in the crowd that he said was a nonbeliever; that he was there to make a joke out of the whole thing; and that he had a bottle of liquor in his inside pocket. All that I saw was the man jumping up and running out of the door. The gentleman continued with me. He said that God wanted him to heal someone in the group tonight as he pointed to me. Being pessimistic, I looked the other way, hoping that he would place his attention on someone else. My aunt said, "Larna, he's pointing to you, get up and go!"

I just sat there until she got up and pulled me from my seat and toward the front to the huge man who was now standing in the middle of the isle. At this point, I continued to just stand there doing nothing. I was so scared I could feel my knees shake. I kept thinking, *What is happening to me? What is he going to do to me or with me?* I'm standing in the middle of the isle now in front of this huge white man who I knew nothing about.

He looked at me like he was seeing everything about me. He took my hand and told me not to look down. That there was nothing but grief and darkness, bad things and sorrow. "Look up to God." So I did look up as I made up my mind to go along with whatever was about to happen.

He (the evangelist) proceeded to say that I had a condition in the lower right hand side of my abdomen and that God wanted it healed. He told me that I had suffered with it for years and that I had told my parents about it, but I was told it was all in my head. That terrible pain was in my head. What this man was telling me, they were all true. I couldn't believe he knew this. How could he know all these things about me? I hadn't told a soul because I didn't want anyone to think that I was crazy, or just believe that it was all in my head, like my parents had told me. He then proceeded by placing his hand on my abdomen and prayed. He said that God was taking the poison out of my body and that I would feel the work of God by a sudden rush of heat when I return to my seat. To this, I didn't know what to do or think, but I said to myself, *Okay! I'll go along with this for now.* He said several more things and sent me back to my chair. I couldn't help thinking what kind of power this man possess to be able to know all my business. Who could he have talked to? There was no one there in Cincinnati that I had mentioned my pain and problems to. How could he have gotten a hold of my parents? No one there at that church knew their number. How could this be happening to me and why? Is it real? Am I dreaming?

He proceeded to talk as he glanced at me from the platform. Slowly, I began to feel a sudden rush of heat. I was getting very warm. That little storefront church had become very hot. Suddenly, I felt like pins were sticking in me. I felt very uncomfortable. I could feel the people looking at me. I was even more determined not to make a spectacle of myself, so I just sit there feeling the surging heat as I wrapped the coat closer around me. I said to myself, *Please don't let this happen to me. This can't be real.* I struggled and struggled with the idea that this was some kind of a prank. At this point, I could no longer take the heat. I threw my coat open and the moisture and heat smoked up the whole church. It seemed at that time. It was huge, a white ball of moisture from the heat of my body. The people around me just let out a sigh of surprise and praise. Till this day, some forty-five years later, I have no pain in that area just like the man from somewhere said. I have looked high and low for the man but I have never heard anything about him. I wished a many day that I had taken my aunt's advice and had taken the time to sit and talk with him when he invited me to do so.

Chapter Seven
Omniscient Word from "God"

Some time had passed since I had done anything that meant something to me. I was depressed. I was in and out of relationships that were going nowhere. It just seemed as through life didn't have much meaning for me and no point to it. I wondered what was my purpose, the purpose for my birth. Why was I put here? What were the reasons for it all? I hadn't accomplished anything that I considered worthwhile. What was it all for?

It was one of those days during the holiday season. I was feeling very low as I often did in those days. I had a friend. He wanted to get married but his actions weren't what I call desirable. I was really wishing for someone with more aggressiveness and honesty, someone more faithful in my relationship. But I felt that maybe this was it for me. Maybe I didn't deserve anyone any better. After all, I'm not a perfect person. So why would I look for someone else to be perfect for me? At any rate, it was one of those relationships. I wanted more, but somehow it didn't seem to work out that way with the men in my life or anything else. It was just another day during the holiday season. We were going to my mother's house, about two and a half hours away from our home. We arrived at my mother's. There was no one there, so John dropped me off and he left. As I entered the house, I noticed that it was completely silent. This made me feel even worse. I was there out in the country all alone. I got more depressed and the thoughts kept running through my mind. I became so depressed that I felt sick to the stomach. It seemed that nothing I tried or attempted paned out for me. I had doubts about the things that I thought about doing and wanted to do. I even questioned God's reason for my being here. What was it all for? Why am I here? Suddenly, with tears in my eyes, I found myself standing in the middle of the room, the living room in my mother's house. It was quiet, still quiet. All of a sudden, from above my head, straight down in front of me fell a piece of paper just floating downward. It was the size of the little papers found in the Chinese fortune cookies. The paper landed at my feet. A spirit spoke to me, saying to me, *"Pick it up."* I did and I held it in my hand and wondered what is this? I looked around me to see where or whom did it come from. But no one was there. A spirit instructed me to read the paper. It said (and I quote) "GOD'S GIFT TO YOU IS WHAT HE HAS GIVEN YOU, AND YOUR GIFT TO GOD IS WHAT YOU MAKE OF WHAT HE HAVE GIVEN YOU!" At that point, I knew that God had a plan, a blueprint for my life. I felt a rush of energy that I can't explain to this day. I set out at that point to fulfill the goals that I have for myself in this life. Again, God has come through, answered my questions, and set me on the right path. Thank you "God."

Chapter Eight
The Voice

Obeying the voice of God can and do help you maintain your life. This particular event happened one day after years of agonizing about whether or not I should stay in the relationship with my friend. It was hard putting up with the women intruding in our lives, not to mention the drinking. It was truly hard having feelings for a person that takes life as a gamble. He was a good-natured man who liked people and liked to have fun, but since coming home from the Vietnam War, he had many demons to deal with. John would drink himself into oblivion, not knowing when to stop, or where he was or what he was doing. I took up with John because I thought that God would bless me if I spent more time helping someone instead of looking for the one who could help me or make me happy. To a certain extent, I still think there is something to the idea even though it didn't quite work out that way for me.

John was nice to me. He treated me good despite his drinking and escapades with other women. He treated me as no other man had up till then. There weren't many in my life, but the few who I knew didn't. John liked people. He was what people call a people person. I was much too shy and introverted to reach out like he did. His family was nice and welcomed me. His family and I spent much time together. I was young and a long way from home. I didn't have the family closeness that John had with his family. Without John, I felt very alone in the large city of Detroit, Michigan.

As time went by, the times that John would drink became unbearable and more frequent. He had a bad habit of drinking and driving. It scared me so much that I would have panic attacks just thinking about it. I often wondered if he would make it home or not. One day, we had an argument. I was bound and determined that this was the end. I had had enough. I couldn't go through this anymore. I prayed. He had stayed out and I didn't see him that day. I sent my son to the babysitter that morning and I went to work. I had planned to call my aunt to pick me up at the dental lab. I then received a call from my babysitter that John had picked up my son who was three years old at the time. She told me that he was coming to pick me up at work. To my surprise, when I got out of work and walked to the parking lot, John and another man was asleep in the car. My son was in there also with the doors locked. Both John and the other man was drunk. They were drunk and I had no money on me to ride the bus or catch a cab. I decided to get the ride home with them. With it being winter, my son being half dressed for the cold, and the darkness soon falling, I prayed and got in the car. I felt it would be best to try to make it home in one piece with John.

As John turned to enter the Southfield Expressway, he just missed the wall. I became very scared and braced myself in the car. I was thinking about my son catching a cold if I got out the car in that weather. As we rode along the expressway, John was so out of control of the car. That's when I heard the voice of God telling me, for the first time, to get out of the car. I wasn't sure of what I had heard or what I should do. *Get out of the car in the middle of the highway. That's insane!* So I sat there, when all of a sudden, the Voice, said: *"Get the baby and get out of the car now!"* In no uncertain terms I understood what was being said. I started to scream for John to stop and let me out. He refused at first, so I kept yelling at him to let me out. I didn't think of what I was going to do next. All I know is that I had to get out of that car now. John pulled over to the side of the highway ramp, and my son and I got out and walked up the ramp to the street above. I had no idea where I was at this point. Every time John took me somewhere, he would take me a different route. I honestly think it was to confuse me in my learning the city. I was thinking, *How will I be able to get home with no money? How will I be able to make a call? Will someone let me use their phone free?* I hope…I was so worried.

I came to the first gas station and asked the attendant. He said that they didn't have a public phone. It was cold, very cold, and it was starting to get dark. I worried about my son and what I had just done. Why hadn't I stayed put in the car in the warmth. At that moment, I heard a very loud bang—more like an explosion—far away. I thought about it a moment and continued on. I figured that by this time I would have been on my way home. I was worried about getting my son home out of the cold and before dark. I hadn't looked in my purse because, the day before, there wasn't anything in it. I had skipped lunch that day. I thought to myself, *What if I got a cab? But how was I going to call a cab with no money?* There was little money at home for emergencies. I had to get home first. I had enough for a cab for such a long ride. I was hoping that it would be enough.

Then the spirit spoke to me again and told me to look in the purse. There was something there. I dug down in my purse, felt a huge bulge (something very thick), and pulled it out. It was my change purse full to the top and sides, bulging with money. I thought to myself, *How did this happen? Where did this come from?* I held it up in the air and looked at it as I thanked my Father in heaven. I had a time making it home. It took a number of different buses to get there. Then when we got to our city and the street that we lived on, the bus did not show up. The evening sun came out and it didn't seem to be as cold. So we walked. By the time we reached home, the bus still had not showed up. I fed and got my son ready for bed. I prayed to God and asked him, *"What shall I do? I can't have my son or myself put in jeopardy like this anymore.* Instantly, God answered my prayer. At that very moment, I was setting at the table just praying and thinking about what to do and what not to do. John suddenly opened the door, walked straight past me to the bedroom, and closed the door. I just sat there wondering, *What do you want me to do God? Please show me a sign, tell me what you want me to do.* I heard a spirit say, *"Look out the window."*

I got up, walked to the window, and looked out. I just stood there looking. The spirit voice instructed me to look down, which I did, and saw the car. The whole front end of the car was in the windshield. The room started to spin and I fell into one of my armchairs that I had by the window. I said, "Thank you, God. Thank you, God." At that time I started to plan my exit from that period in my life to end the relationship and start anew somewhere else.

During my planning period to move away from John with as little abuse and confusion as possible and trying to leave it on a friendly basis, I had a visitor. The man, one of John's colleagues, came to visit. He was the one in the backseat of the car during the wild ride home that night after work. He asked if he could just ask me one question. I said "okay."

"It's about the accident," he said. He said that he had been wondering over and over what made me get out of the car when I did. He said that he just had to know did I hear a voice or something.

Why did I get out the car so fast that day? I told him, "Yes, I did hear a voice telling me to get my son and get out now. I knew at that point that something was about to happen." I told him that he was one hundred percent right, and when I hear the spirit voice speak to me that way, I obey. He said that he will never forget that evening as long as he lives. I said that I know that I won't either.

Chapter Nine
Message from Jimmy

Many years had passed after my brother's death. I had moved to a small town in upper Michigan where I was attending college. I was somewhat happier than I was when living in Detroit. My mother and I were talking about the spiritual side of life when she mentioned to me that she had been told about a church where there were many people like myself. She was telling me that this could help me to understand things better. I found it hard to believe that this existed where I was from. I soon decided to drive down and attend one of the Wednesday night groups. This was something that I was not familiar with. The Rev. Ann call this reading of articles psychometric. It was very mind-boggling to me. My mother put a watch in the article basket, and I put a ring that belonged to my aunt. The session started with prayer and discerning of the spirits. This was to be sure that we are conversing with the spirit of or entity of God and his angels, as there are other types of spirits on the other side.

More outstanding then was when they told me that the message that my mother received was from my brother, Jimmy. He gave my mother advice about her money. Then he told her that the lamb, a planter he had given her the day before his death wasn't on the shelf where she had been keeping it. He said that the day he gave it to her, she promised to keep it for always. To say the least, mother and I were in shock at these words. Mother said that she had not noticed that it wasn't on the shelf. Mother and I just looked at each other as Rev. Ann continued to tell us what little Jimmy's spirit was saying to us. He continued to tell us where the planter was. It was in the little house behind the big house under a long, heavy window attachment.

I couldn't wait to get home to my mother's to see about it all. By the time we got back, it was already after 11:00 PM and very dark. The lights didn't work in the garage, so I couldn't see how to find anything. I couldn't sleep for anticipation. As soon as the sun was on its way up, I was out in the garage, looking for the planter lamb that little Jimmy had given my mother. I found it in the exact spot where my brother said it would be. I took it into the house, cleaned it up, and put it back on the mirror shadow box. That, at the time, was so astonishing for me. It showed the love that the spirit shows from the other side of life. Many things have been shown to me over the years through the Spirit of God. I'm waiting to experience even more in the future.

Chapter Ten
Grandma's Peach Cobbler

It was early February, a cold, snowy winter morning in Michigan. My fiancé, my youngest sister, and my youngest brother decided to go to church. We had a nice service. I decided to get a message from one of the member mediums at the church. It was a good message from my grandmother on my mother's side of the family. The medium asked me, "Did you know that your grandmother was known for her cooking and in the neighborhood?" I told her that I wasn't aware of her being well-known for anything. The medium told me that my grandmother would let me know what it was that she made for the people of the neighborhood. I thought that was interesting and I welcomed the knowledge. Everything went well at the church.

On the way home, we smelt the aroma of a pie while driving down the streets. It seemed as if the smell was getting louder. I asked everyone in the car if they smelt anything. They all said that they smelt something sweet. It smelt like peach cobbler. The smell just got stronger and stronger as we approached the house. We all talked about how good it smelt and that we couldn't wait to taste it. It was so ironic that we could smell this even though we were in a closed car on a very cold winter day in Michigan. It was unbelievable that the smell was so clear. We could all but taste the cobbler coming from someone's house. Why was it smelling so strong? We continued to drive home, still smelling the intense aroma of peach cobbler. As we approached the house and got out of the car, it became dense in the air. We talked about how good it must be.

Inside the house, I headed straight for the kitchen. I asked if anyone else wanted some cobbler. They all said "yes," and that it smells so good. I took the bowls from the cabinets and placed them on the table with the spoons, ready to be served up. I then went to my mother's room to thank her for making the cobbler, telling her that it was just what we needed. I also told my mother how I had been prophesied about my grandma. Mother interrupted me saying that she didn't make a cobbler. I started to laugh and asked her not to joke about it. She looked at me and said once again that she hadn't made a peach cobbler. I looked at her in disbelief. I could not believe what she was saying because I could smell it. We all did! I proceeded back downstairs to the kitchen. I touched the oven—it was cold. Still, I was in disbelief. I opened the oven and saw nothing inside. I went to the living room where the others were waiting and I just looked at them. When I regained my composure, I asked them, "Did you all smell the cobbler?" They replied "yes." I looked and said that there was no peach cobbler in the stove, kitchen, or anywhere in the house. This was a true example of what spirits can do to let us know that God and the angels of God do truly exist.

www.ingramcontent.com/pod-product-compliance
Lightning Source LLC
LaVergne TN
LVHW041601070526
838199LV00046B/2084